Did You Say That?

CAROL E. SIMON-DARANDA, M. ED.

Brief Recall of Some Notable Moments of Humor as
Spoken by Grades K-1 Students from 1992-2016

Did You Say That?

Kids Will Say The Funniest Things

CAROL E. SIMON-DARANDA, M. ED.

WESTBOW
PRESS®
A DIVISION OF THOMAS NELSON
& ZONDERVAN

WestBow Press books may be ordered through booksellers or by contacting:

WestBow Press
A Division of Thomas Nelson & Zondervan
1663 Liberty Drive
Bloomington, IN 47403
www.westbowpress.com
844-714-3454

ISBN: 978-1-6642-1284-8 (sc)
ISBN: 978-1-6642-1283-1 (e)

Print information available on the last page.

WestBow Press rev. date: 11/09/2020

Contents

Dedication

I am sure many K–5 educators can recall moments of laughter in the school setting (the classroom, the playground, the gym, the hallways, the library, the cafeteria, and field trips). Those moments of humor seem to have been precisely timed in that we, the educators, needed a refreshing boost to keep us moving forward. This book consists of language used by kindergartners and other elementary grade students. The honesties and seriousness of their remarks and replies will keep you on your toes in amazement.

This book is dedicated to the many K–5 educators
who experienced their share of gut bursting and knee
slapping laughs during their teaching careers.

Preface

My aunt, Johnnie M. Jones, was an elementary teacher for thirty years. As a child, I recall spending time at Aunt Johnnie's home and listening to her talk about the funny things that her students would do and say. Though I enjoyed those stories, I often thought, is my aunt embellishing those stories to make me laugh and steer me to the field of education? The stories of her students were a motivator for me in becoming a teacher. Aunt Johnnie seemed so happy and was full of pride as she talked about her students. Looking back over my 37 years of teaching, I can truthfully say that I was not disappointed because I too can speak happily and proudly of the many students who I taught over the years. The reasoning behind this work is to share with you the reader bits of humor that I was privileged to enjoy over the many years of my teaching career. I feel privileged to have written this brief work for the following reasons as stated by some of my colleagues of the past:

1. "Carol has a unique manner of academically challenging her students while at the same time entertaining them with her sharp sense of humor."
2. "Ms. Simon is a loving, caring, bright, and talented teacher who takes the time to plan and reach students from varied environments, training them to become independent, productive thinkers of the future who possess a keen sense of humor."

3. "Carol Simon uses everyday practicality in her instruction that is laced with bits of humor to better enable her grasp and maintain ideas and concepts presented."
4. "Carol's creative style of teaching is amazing, and her classroom is buzzing with activities where the students are engaged as her bits of humor makes learning both fun and meaningful."
5. "Carol Simon has a gift of humor that spills and flows to her students and her coworkers."
6. She is jolly, full of life and she is always able to offer a bit of humor to cheer both adult and children alike."
7. "Ms. Simon is serious about her work and the achievement of her students but she also knows the right time to give you a gut busting and knee slapping laugh."
8. "It's amazing how Carol uses that witty sense of hers in the classroom."
9. "Carol is a hoot and the life of the party.
10. "Sitting next to Carol Simon in a meeting is a no-no!"

I chose the title, "Did You Say That? – Kids Will Say the FUNNIEST Things" for this book because there were moments when I could not believe what I heard from my students. I would pause and think, "Now just where or how he or she come up with that statement or question." Children are transparently sincere in their remarks and responses. The words spoken by them are humorous; however they contain common sense and practicality. It was so difficult on some occasions to hold back the laughter. At the kindergarten level they are frank and have not learned the social niceties that lead in some cases to a loss of one's sense of humor. Teaching kindergarten for 37 years has sharpened my sense of humor.

My sincere thanks and appreciation are extended to the following persons:

1. I thank God for 37 years of patience and strength.
2. Aunt Johnnie M. Jones for inspiring me to become an educator
3. My students of 37 years for their wit and humor.
4. My coworkers of 37 years

Introduction

My family was not one which laughed often. My brother Calvin and I were the comedians of the family. Growing up in rural Avoyelles Parish, one had to possess a great sense of humor. Life was difficult back then, because there was always lots of hard work to do, especially the cotton fields. My brother and I made life bearable for our siblings because we could always find the humor in someone or something that helped us to pass the day.

When I became a teacher, my class make up was one of shy children, children with low self-esteem, outgoing children and children who were withdrawn. Within a week or so of interacting with them, I discovered their personality. One thing is true with all children and that is they love to giggle and laugh. I was determined that I would make learning a fun experience for them! When the grasping of new skills and concepts became difficult for them, something humorous would come to my mind that enabled them to relax and catch hold of the concept. To this very day, when I encounter former students, even my first year students, they can recall an incidence of humor we shared. Now, do not you even attempt to go there! Yes, I have seen many moons rise and set)! Evidently, they enjoyed my classroom, because when their children became kindergarten age, there a request list for my class. I instructed, using my sense of humor and shy children, children with low self-esteem, and withdrawn children were molded into life-long productive learners who love a good laugh. Now, who said that pig ears could not be made into a silk purse?

In this book you, the reader, will become acquainted with the language used by kindergarten and other elementary grade students. The humor and honesty of the students will cause your funny button to be activated.

The Watermelon Incidence

Jenea; I am so mad, look at my paper with an S-.

Momma: You had one wrong that's why!

Jenea: No, she said underline the M pictures. So, I underlined the **melon.**

Momma: No, that's **water**melon.

Jenea: Momma, you know we are black people; we don't say, "watermelon," we just say, "melon."

Toast and Butter

Teacher: Underline all the pictures that begin with the letter B.

Jenae: "I did!"

Techer: Why did you underline the toast? Toast begin with the letter T.

Jenae: "I know, but I have butter on my toast.'

All of that Alji and Biop

Jenea's older sister complains about doing algebra and biology.
So, on my way back home

with Jenea she tells me about her day at school. Then she says,
"I'm so tired of all the alji

and biop my teacher gives me every day. All she knows is alji,
biop, alji, biop. I'm

sounding just like Meme in school huh momma/"

Lesson on the Senses (One-on-One)

Teacher: What are your eyes for?

Student: To see with.

Teacher: What are your ears for?

Student; To hear with.

Teacher: What is your nose for?

Student: To dig in!

Where is Mr. Garage?

Pat: Why are you here?

Child: I need to see the principal. My teacher sent me.

Pat: Who do you need to see?

Child: I need to see Mr. **Garage** (Mr. Gerard) the principal.

Rote Teaching

Student: I like school but my teachers not smart at all and don't know much!

Parent: Why?

Student: She never learned her colors. Every day she ask me to tell her the colors of our M&M's candy!

The Flintstone Mobile

Jenea sat and watched me drive one morning. Then she asked, "Momma when you was my age did you have to put your feet on the ground like the Flintstones to make the car go?"

Egg Laying Dogs

Mrs. Simon, Pumba, my cousins' dog, laid 2 puppies last night and when we went to bed and got up, he had laid 8 more in the barn

Babies and Pearls

Sam: I know where babies come from!

Mrs. Simon: Where?

Sam: You get a blue or pink pearl.

Mrs. Simon: From where are the pearls gotten?

Sam: A bird brings you a blue for a boy and a pink for a girl. Then you go to the hospital and pick up the baby!

Sergent

My dog had to have **sergent** (surgery) to keep him from having puppies!

Insex

Mrs. Simon: Class, we will go outside to look for insects.

Mrs. Simon: Where is Lisa?

Class: She already has her sex.

Egg Sitting Snakes

Mrs. Simon: Class, did you know that a snake comes from an egg just as chickens come from eggs?

Child: Now, how can a snake sit on an egg?

The Hairless Chicken

Class: We found a little chicken on the playground and he has lost all his hair!

Mrs. Simon: This is a baby bird, class!

First Week of School and Separation Anxiety

Zachary: I miss my parents so much; I could die on the playground!

Zachary: I want to go home (crying). I don't like coming to school! I miss my parents so much! Mrs. Simon, I want to go home!

Mrs. Simon: Look at me; I know that you miss home; but we all have to stay at school.

Zachary: (walking away and stops the crying) Then he turns says, "OK, thank you!"

Are You Going?

Teacher: Everyone will read a page of their book.

(After 2 or 3 people had finished reading, Alfonso wants to read, because he has memorized the lines, so he begs to read.

Alfonso: I go; you go; we go; I ain't going!

Momma Going Ballistic

Jenea: Momma, we get our papers on tomorrow!

Mother: I know it's on Tuesday; you always get it on that day.

Jenea: When you see these papers, you gonna go ballistics; I know you will! (mother takes papers)

Mother: Jenea, I can't believe you bringing home two U's! Well, we'll see about that!

Jenae: I told you, you'd go ballistics!

Feeling "Weaky"

Teacher: It's time to go outside and paly.

Child: I can't go outside; I feel "weaky!"

My Popeyes

A child holds his arms and says, "Please don't wipe me on my popeyes."

Hiccups and a Pink Elephant

One student had the hiccups. The other one said, "Think about pink elephants."

Deodorant, Lotion
and Ash Wednesday

Mom: Today is Ash Wednesday. It's a Catholic holiday. Oh, by the way did you put on deodorant and lotion?

Jenea: Yes Mama, I put on deodorant; but since it's Ash Wednesday, I don't need any lotion!

Mama and Fat Tuesday

Mama: Today is Fat Tuesday

Jenea: What do we do today?

Mama: Stay home!

Jenea: You have to stay home all day Mama because you fat huh, mama?

Roll Call of Presidents

Roll Call of Students: Present, present, present, president, president

Taking the Baby Everywhere

(Jaquan looking at his pregnant play mom) Momma Meme, you are a good momma; you carry the baby everywhere you go huh?

Pissatating

Teacher: Where are the papers mom was supposed to sign and send back to school?

Child: My momma said, "I can't pissatate (participate) in nothing!

Teacher: You can't what?

Child: I can't pissatate (participate) until I get a better conduct grade.

Teacher: OK!

Cauliflower, Indians and Ships

After three or four days of discussion on the first Thanksgiving, I decided to ask questions on what we had learned.

Teacher; What was the name of the people who traveled on the big ship?

Students' Answers: The players, the people, the Pilgrims

Teacher: Who were the people they saw?

Students: The Indians

Teacher: How many people were on the ship?

Students' Answers: 3,000, 400

Teacher: There were hundreds of people!

Student: One hundred two (102) to one hundred ninety (190).

Teacher: Good! Now, the big ship had a name. What was the name of the big ship they traveled on?

Students: The Califlower (Mayflower).

No Constructions

Child: Thank you for my toy!

Grandmother: What did you get?

Child: I don't know yet. I have to put it together. Well, you know there're no constructions (instructions) on how to put it together in the box!

Grandmother: No constructions (instructions)?

The Next Day is Tomorrow

Child: I coming to see you on Monday, Tuesday, and Friday, all the week "DD?"

Grandmother; You know how to say the days of the week in order? What comes after Monday?

Child: Tuesday

Grandmother: What comes after Tuesday?

Child: (pauses)

Grandmother: What comes after Tuesday?

Child: Tomorrow!

Maddome

Child: My Mama cut her hair last night. She looks just like Maddome (Madonna).

My Grandmother

(Jenea and her friend were talking about their grandmothers)

Jenea: I am going to visit my grandmother this weekend.

Friend: I go to visit my grandma too.

Friend: What's your grandma's name?

Jenea: My grandmother is Mrs. Spruill.

Friend: She can't be your grandmother.

Jenea: Why she can't be my grandmother?

Friend: Because Mrs. Spruill is white and you are black.

Jenea: Well, she can't help that.

About the Writer

Carol Elaine Williams Simon-Daranda was born in Marksville, Louisiana. She is one of 7 children born to Lawrence (Tee) Williams and Murline Simon-Williams.

Her grade school and high school years were spent at Mary Bethune High School of Marksville, Louisiana. Carol graduated from Northwestern State University of Natchitoches with a degree in Early Childhood and Elementary Education and from Southern University of Baton Rouge, Louisiana with a Masters in Elementary Education. She retired from the Avoyelles Parish School System in 2014 after 38 years of teaching.

She was selected for "Teacher of the Year" on two occasions at Lafargue Elementary School. Carol won Elementary Level "Teacher of the Year" for Avoyelles Parish. These were very humbling experiences for her, as she was selected based upon her coworkers recommendations.

Carol has been married to Sylvester Daranda of Houston, TX for 6 years. She is the proud mother of two daughters (Megan and Erin) and six grandchildren (Xavier, Jakhirian, Tro'Una, LaPatrick, Troy and Troylee).

Printed in the United States
By Bookmasters